PIANO • VOCAL • GUITAR

THE VERY BEST OF
the Rat Pack

ISBN 978-1-61780-356-7

HAL•LEONARD®
CORPORATION

7777 W. BLUEMOUND RD. P.O. BOX 13819 MILWAUKEE, WI 53213

Visit Hal Leonard Online at
**www.halleonard.com**

# COME FLY WITH ME

Words by SAMMY CAHN
Music by JAMES VAN HEUSEN

# AIN'T THAT A KICK IN THE HEAD

Words by SAMMY CAHN
Music by JAMES VAN HEUSEN

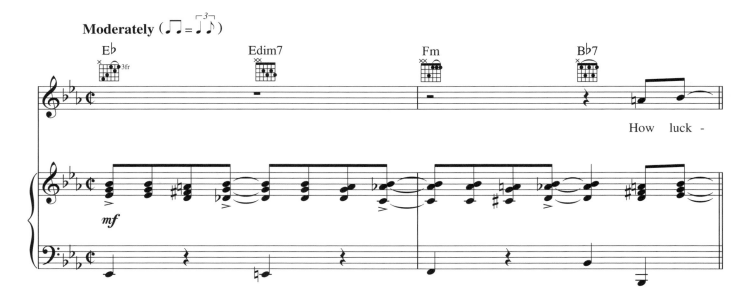

# TOO CLOSE FOR COMFORT
## from the Musical MR. WONDERFUL

Words and Music by JERRY BOCK,
LARRY HOLOFCENER and GEORGE WEISS

16

# I'VE GOT YOU UNDER MY SKIN

## from BORN TO DANCE

Words and Music by
COLE PORTER

Fm7♭5  B♭7  D  E♭maj7  E♭6

fair   nev - er   will   go   so   well." _____   But

Dm7   G7   Cdim7   C

why should I   try   to re - sist   when, dar - ling,   I   know   so   well? _____

A♭6   A♭m6/B♭   B♭7   E♭maj7

_____   I've   got   you _____   un - der   my   skin. _____

E♭6   Fm7/E♭   B♭7/E♭

_____   I'd   sac - ri - fice   an - y - thing,   come   what might, for   the

# WHO'S GOT THE ACTION?

Words and Music by GEORGE DUNING
and JACK BROOKS

# A LOT OF LIVIN' TO DO

## from BYE BYE BIRDIE

Lyric by LEE ADAMS
Music by CHARLES STROUSE

# RING-A-DING DING

Words by SAMMY CAHN
Music by JAMES VAN HEUSEN

# EEE-O ELEVEN

Words by SAMMY CAHN
Music by JAMES VAN HEUSEN

**Slow and bluesy**

Some-day I'll ___ have ___ me a chauf-feur and a block-long ___ lim-ou-sine; eee-o e-lev-en, eee-o ___ e-lev-en. Some-day I'll ___ have ___ me a pent-house, stacks and

# LUCK BE A LADY
## from GUYS AND DOLLS

By FRANK LOESSER

# VOLARE
## (Nel blu, dipinto di blu)

Music by DOMENICO MODUGNO
Original Italian Text by D. MODUGNO and F. MIGLIACCI
English Lyric by MITCHELL PARISH

Some-times the world is a val-ley of heart-aches and tears,
*Pen - so che un so - gno co - sì non ri - tor - ni mai più:*

and in the hus-tle and bus-tle no sun-shine ap-
*mi di - pin - ge - vo le ma - ni e la fac - cia di*

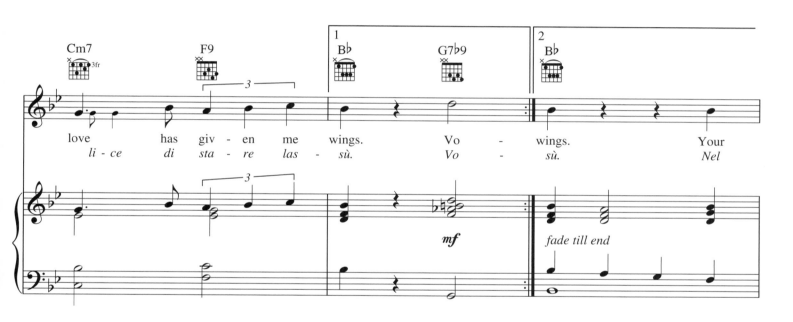

# THE BIRTH OF THE BLUES
## from GEORGE WHITE'S SCANDALS OF 1926

Words by B.G. DeSYLVA and LEW BROWN
Music by RAY HENDERSON

# WITCHCRAFT

Music by CY COLEMAN
Lyrics by CAROLYN LEIGH

# YOU'RE NOBODY 'TIL SOMEBODY LOVES YOU

Words and Music by RUSS MORGAN,
LARRY STOCK and JAMES CAVANAUGH

# I GET A KICK OUT OF YOU

from ANYTHING GOES

Words and Music by
COLE PORTER

# SAM'S SONG

Words by JACK ELLIOTT
Music by LEW QUADLING

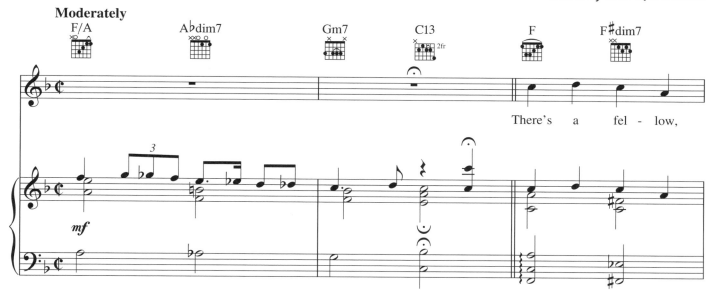

# I'M GONNA LIVE TILL I DIE

Words and Music by AL HOFFMAN,
WALTER KENT and MANNY KURTZ

# EVERYBODY LOVES SOMEBODY

Words by IRVING TAYLOR
Music by KEN LANE

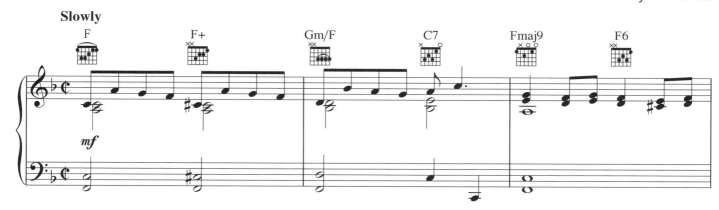

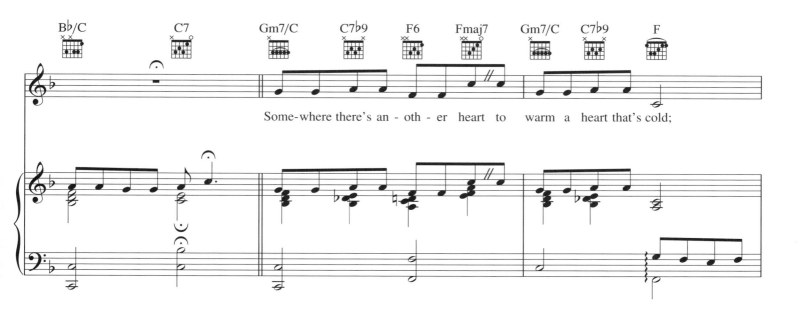

Some-where there's an-oth-er heart to warm a heart that's cold;

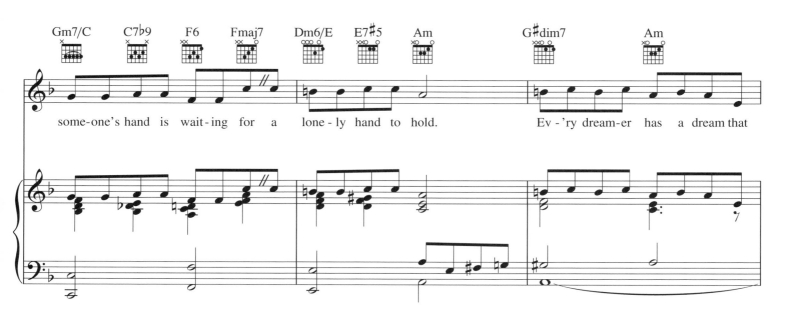

some-one's hand is wait-ing for a lone-ly hand to hold. Ev-'ry dream-er has a dream that

# ME AND MY SHADOW

Words by BILLY ROSE
Music by AL JOLSON and DAVE DREYER